SHAKESPEARE MUSIC

Da Capo Press Music Reprint Series
GENERAL EDITOR
FREDERICK FREEDMAN
VASSAR COLLEGE

SHAKESPEARE MUSIC

(Music of the Period)

Edited by E. W. Naylor

DA CAPO PRESS · NEW YORK · 1973

Library of Congress Cataloging in Publication Data

Naylor, Edward Woodall, 1867-1934, ed.
  Shakespeare music.

  (Da Capo Press music reprint series)
  Reprinted from the 2d ed. of 1927.
  1. Shakespeare, William, 1564-1616—Musical settings.
I. Title.
M1619.S52N33   782.8'3'0942   75-171080
ISBN 0-306-70275-4

This Da Capo Press edition of *Shakespeare Music* is an
unabridged and slightly corrected republication of the
second edition published *c.* 1927. It is reprinted by
special arrangement with J. Curwen & Sons, Ltd.

Published by Da Capo Press, Inc.
A Subsidiary of Plenum Publishing Corporation
227 W. 17th Street, New York, New York 10011

SHAKESPEARE MUSIC

Shakespeare Music

(Music of the Period)

(Curwen Edition 8294)

Edited by

E. W. Naylor, Mus.D.

Second Edition

London:
J. Curwen & Sons Ltd.,
24 Berners Street, W.1

London:
George Allen & Unwin Ltd.,
Ruskin House,
40 Museum Street, W.C.1

U.S.A.:
Curwen Inc.,
Germantown, Philadelphia

PREFACE.

ALL the arrangements of old tunes in this collection are entirely new, and are intended to be useful in the production of Shakespeare and contemporary plays; it is also hoped that they will convey sound instruction in the actual features of music in Shakespeare's time.

As it would be unpardonable impertinence to give the public modern paraphrases of Shakespeare to read, instead of Shakespeare's own words, so is it unpardonable to allow people to hear or to use arrangements of old music which misrepresent it by the addition of impossible harmonies, or by modifications of the melodies, intended to make them rather more like the music of our own day. Every effort has been made to render this collection trustworthy in such respects.

In order to prevent misunderstanding, I wish to say that the book does not include every surviving contemporary setting of "Shakespeare" songs. Such a complete collection would be a very small affair, and not particularly useful. My aim has been to give Shakespeare students a correct idea of music as Shakespeare himself knew it.

The plan of the book (see Table of Contents) has been to take the plays in which most music occurs, and give the contemporary music complete (as far as possible) for those plays. On this plan a well-known song like "O mistress mine" is included, being one of a large number of musical pieces in one play; but an equally well-known song, Desdemona's "Song of Willow," is omitted, there being hardly any music at all in "Othello." It seemed unnecessary, again, to print such a familiar song as "Tak thy auld cloak about thee," merely because Iago sings an odd verse of it in Act II ("King Stephen was a worthy peer"). On the other hand, I have thought it right to give "Come o'er the bourn, Bessy," although there is so little music in "Lear," simply because it is practically unknown.

With regard to instrumental music, I have decided not to print any "Fancies," because I am sure no one would use them, dry and dull for the most part as they are.

PREFACE—continued. ·

I wish to draw special attention to the various ways in which the instrumental pieces may be performed, more or less perfectly, so as to give a fair idea of what would be heard in Shakespeare's time. An instance of what I have tried to do is in "Heart's Ease," which can be played in no less than eight ways, according to the facilities available.

I may also point out the considerable number of pieces which are probably published now for the first time: _e.g._, Kemp's Jigg, p. 28; The Hamburgh March, p. 30; the Pavane for Cittern by Strogers,* p. 55; and Ophelia's songs, pp. 36-40, here given in a form in which they can be used.

The vocal pieces on pp. 64 and 63, by King Henry VIII and his contemporary, William Cornysshe, the Master of the Children of the Chapel Royal, 1509 to about 1523, will serve to introduce many to the music of pre-Elizabethan days.

CAMBRIDGE, SEPTEMBER, 1912.

* A literal transcription of this Pavane has been printed in "The Musical Antiquary" of April, 1910 (Henry Frowde), as an illustration of my article on "Music and Shakespeare."

INDEX.

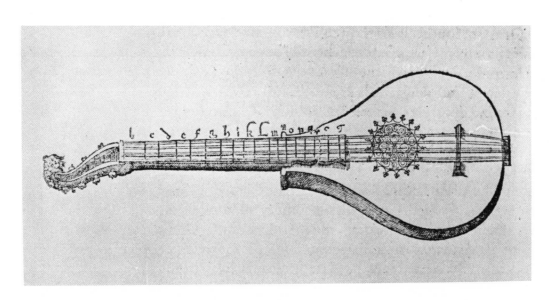

Cittern

[*See pages* 42, 55.

Photograph of the engraving in the *Harmonicorum Instrumentorum* of Mersenne (1), published Paris, 1636.

Notice the four double strings, the eight pegs, the eighteen frets, marked from 'b' to 't,' 18 semitones; and the lion's face on the head.

(1) Père Mersenne, born 1588, was a student of theology, mathematics, and music. Amongst his friends were such distinguished men as Descartes, Pascal *père*, and Huyghens. He lived in Paris. Died 1648.

8294

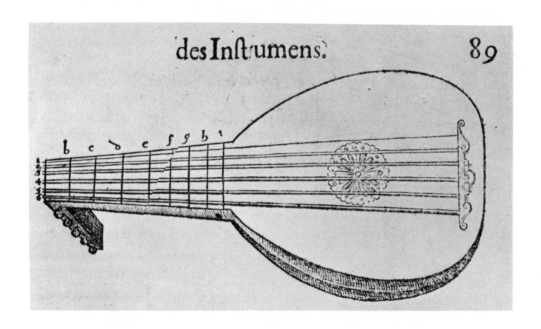

Lute

[*See pages* 28–30, 52.

Photograph from Mersenne (Paris, 1636). This is just the ordinary Lute, with 11 strings, tuned to the six notes given in the 'Heart's Ease' explanation. The single string (uppermost in this picture) was G on line 2 of treble clef. Notice eight frets, marked 'b' to 'i'. Five out of the eleven pegs are visible.

8294

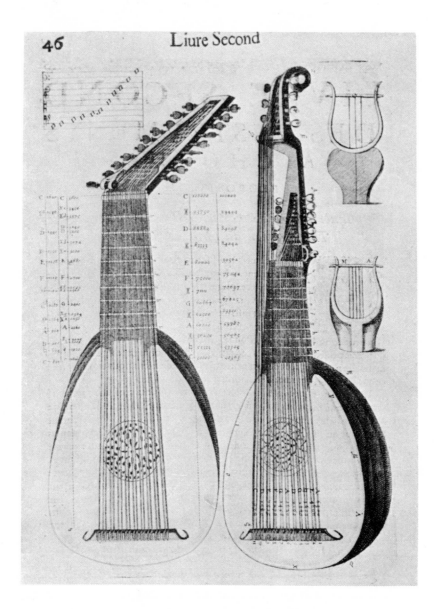

Theorbo and Archlute

Photograph from the engraving in Mersenne (Paris, 1636).

Notice the 19 strings, and pegs to correspond, in the one; and the double head of the other, the lower with 13 pegs, the upper with 8, total 21 strings. In both, notice the 9 semitonal frets, marked from 'b' to 'k'. Also the tuning, with its curious use of the clefs, *e.g.* the F clef at the top *means* F on the 1st space of treble clef. The lowest four notes, C D E F, under bass staff, are those of the 8 strings in the upper peg-box of the instrument on the right. The other, on the left, is engraved wrongway on, looking-glass fashion.

[*See page* 1.

Heart's ease (the name is at the *end* of the tune).

Photograph of a page in MS., Lute Book at Cambridge (Dd. ii. 11). The tune begins in the middle of line 2, and ends where the name 'Hartes ease' is written.

Eight bars of the Lute tablature in modern type.

etc.

The 6 lines ≡≡≡ represent the 6 pitches to which the strings of the Lute are tuned. These pitches vary, but the most usual method is to have the lowest tuned to G, the bottom line of the bass stave, and the highest to 'g' on the second line of the treble stave; the others being tuned in fourths upwards from the one, and downwards from the other—

6 5 4 3 2 1

1 is a single string ; 2, 3, 4, 5, 6 are double strings ; total, 11 strings.

The letters a, b, c, d, e, f, etc., indicate successive semitones on each string. The first, 'a', is really the 'nut', *i.e*, 'a' means, pluck the string with no fingering; or, as violinists say, use the 'open' string; 'b' means the first fret, making the string sound a semitone higher; 'c', two semitones higher; and so on.

Thus, to take the melody, the first letter in bar 1, top string, is 'a'. That is the 'open' string, and *sounds* treble 'g'; the next letter is 'c', the second fret, *sounding* a tone higher than 'g', *viz.* 'a'; the first letter in bar 2 is 'e', the fourth fret, *sounding* 'b natural'; and so on. Take the chord of 6 notes in bar 8; the two top strings are 'a', and the bottom one also 'a'; these require no fingering; the other three are all 'c', that is, they require one finger on the second fret. This big chord then is quite easy to play.

The tails and hooks of quavers, semiquavers, and demisemiquavers, above the music, tell the rhythm and the time, ⌐ = a minim, ⌐ = a crotchet, ⌐ = a quaver, the 'dot' has the usual meaning. A semibreve, when it happens, is indicated simply by an upright stroke |

Hartes ease.

[Heart's ease.]

Romeo and Juliet, IV. 5. 102.

From " Cambridge Lute Book," .MS., Dd, ii. 11.

Trans. E. W. NAYLOR (March 26, 1912).

I, II, VI are the numbers of the strings, to show the student something of the fingering.

See *Taming of the Shrew*, ii. 1. 151, *e.g.*, at VI, last bar but 3, it is only by a good deal of inconvenient twisting that the left hand can reach an F♯ to complete that chord; and even the bass D has to be played on the VIth string, seven frets up.   (See *Shrew, id.*, line 153.)

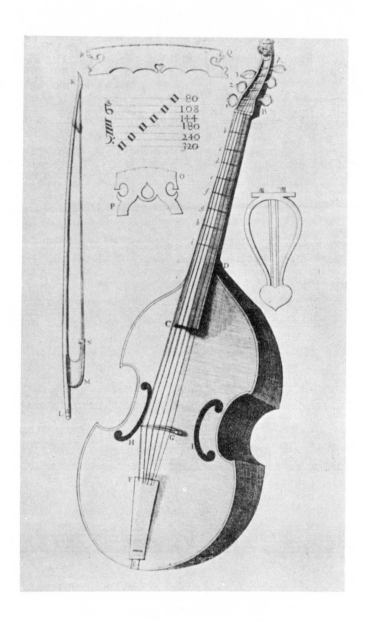

Viol da Gamba and Bow

[*See page* 40.

From Mersenne (Paris, 1636). Notice the curves of the shoulders and waist, unlike violin or violoncello, but like those of double bass (the only survivor of the viols). Also the more primitive bow, and the frets 'b' to 'h'. The tuning is given as usual; the lowest note, D under bass staff. The clefs are to be read an octave lower. The figures (80, 108, etc.) are measures of length, showing how to get these particular notes on one string, *e.g.*, the lowest string, D, is marked 320, and the highest string D *two octaves higher* (D over bass staff), is marked 80, *i.e.* a quarter of 320. A similar set of figures may be seen in the Lute picture.

8294

Part. I.   *The Division Violist.*

Man Playing Viol da Gamba   [*See page* 40.

Photograph from Christopher Sympson's *Division Violist* (London 1659). Sympson was a soldier in the Civil War, on the King's side. This picture shows how to hold the bow, viz. thumb over, not under, the nut; another point of resemblance to the double bass method.

8294

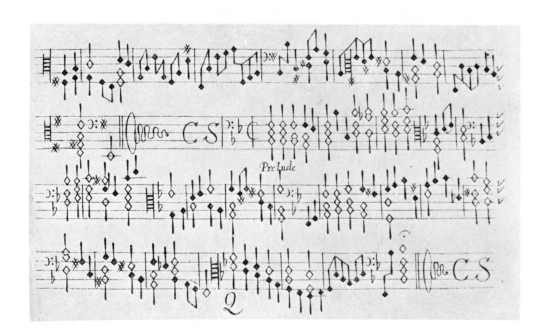

Prelude for Viol da Gamba

From Christopher Sympson's *Division Violist* (London 1659). C. S. shows that Sympson himself is the composer. This piece makes plain how freely chords and double-notes could be played on the *six*-stringed viol. Hardly any of this piece can be played on a violoncello, simply because the *four* strings will not do it.

8294

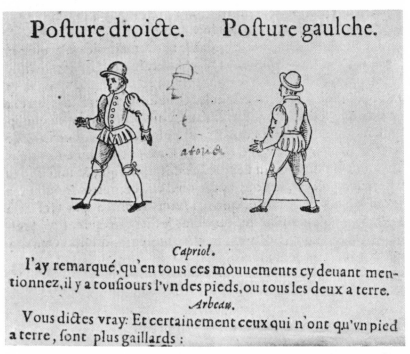

'Postures'

[*See page* 12.

Photograph of the engraving in Arbeau's *Orchésographie*, a treatise on Dancing, published at Langres. There is no date on the title-page, but the official permission to print the work, at the end of the book, gives date Nov. 22, 1588.

There is a modern reprint, Paris, 1888, and a German version, with the music and pictures, by Czerwinski, Danzig, 1878.

The 'Greve'

[*See page* 12.

Photograph from Arbeau, 1588. (See the other picture from the same work.)

An Elizabethan Wedding Feast

A portion of a large picture representing incidents in the life of Sir Henry Unton.

See the description opposite.

Part of a large picture in the National Portrait Gallery, representing various incidents in the life of Sir Henry Unton, an Elizabethan gentleman. The picture was painted in the last years of the sixteenth century, and this particular portion of it shows Sir H. Unton's wedding feast.

The family and the guests are seated at the table. Observe the sideboard, covered with plate; also the several men servants. Likewise the fact that gentlemen at table are wearing their hats.

On the same level as the table, to the left, is a small "consort", which appears to consist of four viols and a boy who is probably singing a song to their accompaniment.

The four men sitting round the small table below are very likely going to sing a quartet or join in the chorus to the boy's song. It is remarkable that there is nothing to drink on this table.

Underneath the marriage feast, solemnly marching up the stairs, and so into the dining-room, is the Masque. The "persons" include Mercury (the black boy with wings and a white hat, also winged), Diana (notice the crescent on top of her headdress, and the flat mask on her face), and alternate pairs of masked ladies and children dressed in black and white, the black presenting the Hours of Night, the white the Hours of Day. These children carry torches. The drummer on the right is keeping time for the procession which is now out of hearing of the "consort" below. This consort includes a flute (transverse, not a recorder), a treble viol, a bass viol, a lute, a cittern, and another instrument of the lute sort (played by the man with his back turned to the spectator).

So we find that this wedding employed ten instrumentalists, or eleven if we count the drummer, and five singers; total, sixteen.

8294

CONTENTS

8294

ROMEO AND JULIET.

Heart's Ease.

Romeo and Juliet, Act. iv., sc. 5, after Juliet's apparent death. Peter asks the musicians to play "Heart's ease." He calls the players by nicknames, viz., Catling (small gut string), Rebeck (ancient three-stringed fiddle), Soundpost (the upright which stands under the right hand foot of a violin bridge, inside the instrument). These three men, who had come to play at the wedding, were fiddlers. I therefore give the tune arranged for violins, in the style customary in Shakespeare's time for the viols.

E. W. N.
Date of tune, before 1560.

① The Cambridge Lute Book has this little variant here, MS., Dd ii, 11, p. 84—

② The Alternative small notes in Violin 3, are to be used only when the violoncello or pianoforte takes part, to avoid octaves with the bass.

8294

CURWEN

CURWEN

This tune may be played in eight ways: (1) violins 1 and 2 alone; (2) all three violins alone; (3) violin 1 and pianoforte; (4) violins 1 and 2 with pianoforte; (5) all three violins with pianoforte; (6) the three violins, with a violoncello, which simply plays the bass of the pianoforte part; (7) three violins, violoncello, and pianoforte; (8) if there is a flute available, or a flageolet, it should play the part of violin 1, instead of the violin, in any or all of these cases. This would be *broken music* (see *Troilus and Cressida*, Act iii, sc. i, l. 52, and *Henry V.*, Act v, sc. 2, l. 248), because the flute is a different sort of instrument from the violin. Arrangements (3), (4), (5), and (7) would also have this name, because of the introduction of a keyed instrument. The arrangements including violins alone

viz., (1), (2), (6), would be called *whole consorts*. If there is a viola it can play the part of violin 3 exactly as it stands. When there is a violoncello, the pianoforte, if used, should play the bass an octave lower, and not too loud. There is a picture in the National Portrait Gallery, reproduced on p. xvi, of Sir Henry Unton's marriage feast, showing the band, or *Broken Consort*, consisting of several sorts of instruments—viol, flute, drum, lute, etc.

The same Peter, a little later in the same scene (*Romeo and Juliet*, Act iv, sc. 5, l. 125) quotes the following song by Richard Edwards, who died in 1566. It is originally for four voices. I have arranged it as a song with pianoforte accompaniment.

In praise of Music.

Arr. E.W.N.
R. EDWARDS. d. 1566.

4

Da Capo al 𝄋

There Mu - sic with her sil - ver sound
The care - ful head re - lief hath found
Of Mu - sic whom the Gods as - signed

Is wont with speed to give re - dress.
By Mu - sic's pleas - ant sweet de - lights;
To com - fort man, whom cares would nip.

Of trou - bled minds for ev - er - y sore, Sweet
Our sen - ses, what should I say more, Are
Sith thou both man and beast dost move, What

Mu - sic hath a salve in store.
sub - ject un - to Mu - sic's lore.
wise man then will thee re - prove?

The original 3rd verse is omitted

CURWEN

The "doleful dumps" of Richard Edward's 1st verse follow easily from Peter's request to the musicians to play a "merry *dump* to comfort me."—*Romeo and Juliet,* iv, 5, 105. Here is a dump, such as they might have played on this occasion. It is not "merry." Peter calls it so in joke. The "dump" was a slow doleful dance, see Shake-speare's *Lucrece,* line 1127. "Distress likes *dumps,* when time is kept with tears." I give the version printed by Stainer and Barrett, with additional small notes by myself. I have tried to find the source used by Stainer, but have failed to trace it.

My Lady Carey's Dump.

Arr. E. W. N.
Date about 1600. (Stainer and Barrett.)

① Observe the signature, only *one* flat, although nowadays we should use *two*. The E flats are all accidentals therefore. When Handel wrote the *Messiah* it was still the custom, in minor keys, to have one flat less than in the modern system.

8294

CURWEN

CURWEN

This Dump may be played in four ways: (1) on the pianoforte alone, in the form given by Stainer, omitting all the small notes; (2) on the pianoforte alone, adding the small notes; (3) as a *trio* for violin, viola, and violoncello (the viola can play *both* the inner parts of the last four bars, and all the small notes in r.h. stave where he has nothing in l.h.);

(4) as a string quartet: the 2nd violin part is indicated by the small notes in r.h. stave, and occasionally in l.h. stave, where there is no tenor part in large notes.

Here follows the true original, of the early 16th century, from the little oblong MS. in British Museum.

My Lady Carey's Dompe.

From British Museum, Royal M S. Appendix 58. Fol. 44 b.

The necessary sharps are placed over the line. Those in the stave are actually in the M S.

Date 1510.

The small notes in staves 4 and 5 are mine, and are certainly intended by the composer. The missing bar and three-quarters (p. 8, top line), also in small notes, was observed by John Stafford Smith. The bass in the MS. from here is in confusion, but it is obvious what is meant.

Final bar wanting in MS.

This very old piece of music for Virginals has a singular affinity with the Nocturne of Chopin and Field 400 years later! The student may be referred to, for instance, Chopin, Op. 37, No. 1. It might be used in *Two Gentlemen of Verona*, Act iv, sc. 2, as part of the Silvia Serenade. See Act iii, sc. 2, line 85. Proteus's friends were singers and players both. They might play the "deploring dump," and then sing W. Cornysshe's "Ah, the sighs," the last piece but one in this book. In the Fitzwilliam Virginal Book, however, we find the *Irish Dump*, and this is just as cheerful as "Lady Carey's Dump" is mournful. Here it is arranged for two violins alone, or with pianoforte if desired.

The Irish Dump.

Arr. E. W. N.
Date probably 16th. Century.

TWELFTH NIGHT.

Shakespeare's *Twelfth Night* is full of music. The Duke's first lines, which begin the play, might be accompanied by Lady Carey's Dump, or part of it, arranging for the Duke to begin his speech in section 2; he should stop and listen to section 3, played only once, and speak again at the *pp* in section 4—"that strain again, it had a dying fall"—when the musicians would stop and repeat the whole sentence from the *p* in section 4, exaggerating the expression of the *pp* phrase, then waiting till the Duke says "Oh, it came o'er my ear," etc., then continuing to play up to the end of the *f* passage, when the Duke would say, "Enough, no more," etc. Another very suitable piece would be Orlando Gibbons' Pavan called—

The Lord of Salisbury His Pavin.

Published 1611 in "Parthenia." ✛
The ornaments are mostly omitted.

ORLANDO GIBBONS, b. 1583.

✛ The work "Parthenia" is a collection of pieces for the *virginals*; so the best we can do is to play the piece on the pianoforte, unless a *harpsichord* can be had, which is practically the same as the virginals. This piece may conveniently be played as a *violin solo*, the pianoforte simply playing everything *except the melody*.

CURWEN

STRAIN III.

I have made some very slight re-arrangements of the parts.—E. W. N. The last 8 bars well present the "dying fall" in the Duke's speech.—*Twelfth Night*, Act. i, sc. 1, line 4.

CURWEN

This Pavan of Orlando Gibbons, though somewhat over-elaborated for the purpose, may be used for dancing. Each semibreve has a step. Jehan Tabourot, best known as Thoinot Arbeau (an anagram of his real name which appears in his book on dancing, "Orchésographie," 1588, Langres) explains these steps as "two simples and a double" advancing, and "two simples and a double" retiring. A "simple" means *left foot forward* at semibreve 1, and *bring right foot up to the left again* at semibreve 2; so "two simples" means further that at semibreve 3 the dancer *advances his right foot*, and at semibreve 4 *brings his left foot up again*; "et ainsi sera parfaict le mouvement des deux simples." The feet merely slip along the floor, there is no springing or bouncing about; and Arbeau particularly advises the dancer to suit the length of his steps to the size of the room, and remember that the lady cannot be supposed to take such long steps as her masculine partner. The "double" is equally easy to explain. At semibreve 1, *advance left foot*; at semibreve 2, *advance right foot*; at semibreve 3, *advance left foot*; and at semibreve 4, *join right foot to left*. Then repeat till the music is finished. The total result of these genteel movements would be a very slow and stately progress along the floor and so round the room; the "two simples" leave the dancer where he starts, but the "double" moves him along a couple of yards or so. Hence Beatrice in *Much Ado about Nothing*, Act ii, sc. 1, line 76, compares the Pavan (which she calls "measure") with a stately wedding procession. Hence also Sir Toby's remarks to Sir Andrew, *Twelfth Night*, Act i, sc. 3, line 126, where he speaks of "going to *church* in a Galliard," the galliard being a comparatively sedate dance in triple time, which always followed the Pavan (or measure), and included amongst its "steps" just one *leap* or *caper*;

thus Sir Toby's idea of a tolerably serious dance, one fit to "go to church" with, was a Galliard. It should be remembered, that though the *movements* of a Galliard were violent, the *time* had to be slow; slower than that of a Tourdion *par terre*, for instance.

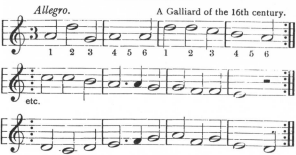

This may be played on any tin whistle, making the last note *Re*. Thus the first note will have all holes open except the top hole. This would sound not unlike the tabor pipe, usually played at dances in 16th century.

The six movements, comprising five "steps" (hence the name *Cinque pas*, or *Sinkapace*) and one "leap" (hence the name *La Volta*) are (1) Greve gaulche, (2) Greve droicte, (3) Greve gaulche, (4) Greve droicte, (5) Sault majeur, (6) Posture gaulche. Greve = coup de pied or "a blow of the foot"; gaulche=left; droicte=right. Sault majeur is the leap at step 5. The second six minims are the *Revers*, *i.e.*, right and left change places.

Here is "Anthoinette" arranged for a common 6-holed whistle *made in the key of F*. The holes will not easily provide accidentals, so the pure Dorian scale will be preserved.

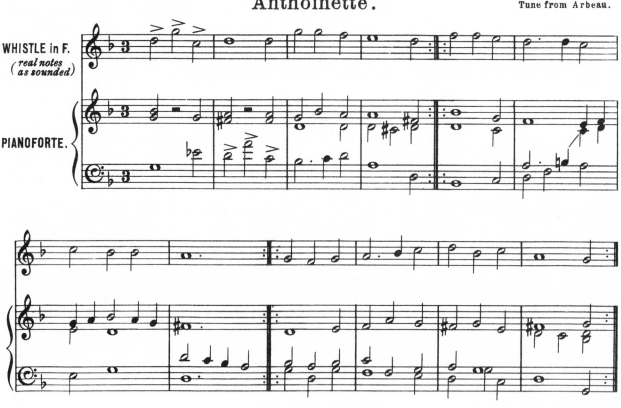

The tune begins on *la* and ends on *re*. Of course, a violin may play the tune instead of a whistle, or a real flute. If a string quartet is available, the four parts are easily copied from the above, which is written in pure 16th century harmony, for that purpose. If a *flute* plays the melody, and a *violin*, a *viola*, and *violoncello* the other three parts, that will be like what Shakespeare would call *Recorder* and *Viols*, a "broken consort," the *Recorder* being a flute with a whistle mouth. See Shakespeare, in *Hamlet*, Act iii, sc. 2, line 346, where the band of musicians enter with the "recorders." There may have been four of them, of four different sizes, and would play the above Galliard on the four, as it stands. This would be a "whole consort," all the instruments being of one sort. In the third scene of *Twelfth Night*, where Sir Toby tries to get Sir Andrew to show off his dancing, Sir Toby might sing the tune of "Anthoinette" for Sir Andrew to display his accomplishment, thus Sir Toby: "Let me *see* thee caper" (Sir Andrew dances). Sir Toby sings noisily—

Lal lal lal *la* ✻ la, Lal lal lal *la* ✻ la.
"Ha! higher."

Lal lal lal la ✻ le la lal lal lal la. ✻
"Ha! ha! excellent!"

Exeunt. [The "capers" happen at ✻.]

The other dances proposed by Sir Toby to Sir Andrew are the Coranto and the Jig. (The "Sinkapace" has already been explained as a name for the Galliard.) Here is a simple *Coranto* from Arbeau, which may be played on the penny whistle in F as above. Begin on *re*.

Coranto.
Harmony by E.W.N.

The figures 1—8 show where the steps belong, as follows: 1, 2, simple gauche, *i.e.*, *left foot* out at 1, and join right foot up at 2; 3, 4, simple droit, *i.e.*, *right foot* out at 3, and join left foot up at 4; 5—8 same as 1, 2, twice over; thus it is the same sort of dance as the Pavan or Measure, but much faster. That is why Sir Toby suggests the more restrained Galliard to "go to church," and the Coranto to "come home."

The Jig of Shakespeare's time was not like the Gigue of later days, viz., written in 6-8 time, with a rhythm of ♩ ♪ ♪ ♪. It was a quick 4-4 dance, *e.g.*—

The Cobbler's Jig.
Harmony by E.W.N.
Date 1622.

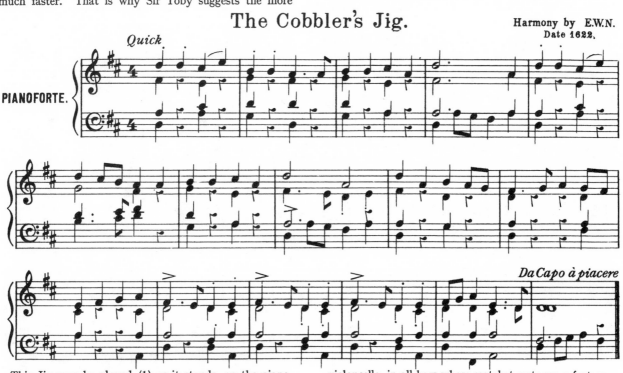

This Jig may be played (1) as it stands, on the pianoforte; (2) on violin, which takes the melody, accompanied by the pianoforte playing the remainder of the parts; (3) as string quartet, using *pizzicato* for vl. 2, viola, and violoncello, in all bars where crotchet rests are a feature— the vl. 1 would, of course, play the tune all through *col arco*; (4) on a whistle, beginning on the upper *do*.

① The whistle cannot play F♯: so the pianoforte must make it F♮, when accompanying.

CURWEN

Act ii, sc. 3, of *Twelfth Night* uses or mentions no less than seven vocal numbers, viz., six songs and one Catch.

O Mistress Mine.

Sung by the CLOWN.

Accompt. by E.W.N.

The accompaniment of this song can be easily written out for string quartet. Notice the way the 2nd violin and viola cross each other; this is a common feature of the old music for viols. Also the little "imitation" of the melody in the 2nd violin, at "journeys' end" which is a good illustration of what was often done in Elizabethan madrigals (for voices) or fancies (instrumental).

CURWEN

Sir Toby now proposes, Act ii, sc. 3, line **58**, to sing a Catch, which he says will wake the owls up, and draw three souls out of one weaver. This is a really good joke, and means that Sir Toby understood all about Catch singing. *Weavers*, and other men of trades which led to sitting indoors three or four at a time, like tailors, cobblers, etc., were fond of singing Catches. Sir Toby's description of the art as "drawing *three souls* out of *one weaver*" is a clever allusion to the way in which the *three-part harmony* is produced by *one melody*.

Thou Knave.

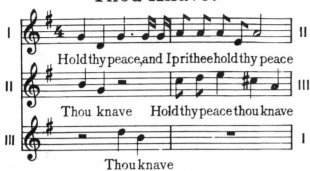

The Clown begins (see line **69**) and I think Sir Toby would come next, as Sir Andrew was a feeble person, and both the Clown and Sir Toby sharp enough to know that the catch really can be sung by *two* voices only; so they would be independent of their incompetent friend.

The following are much better catches, and Shakespeare would know all of them.

Ding dong bell.

Printed 1609.

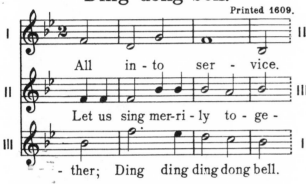

This is the sort Falstaff would like, for he was fond of singing, and of cathedral singers. See *Henry IV*, Part II, Act i, sc. 2, l. **182**, and Act ii, sc. 1, l. **88**. Also *Henry IV*, Part I, Act ii, sc. 4, l. **137**, and *id*., sc. 2, line **43**.

A specimen which really is intended for four voices, though three would do at a pinch, and is of great interest, being actually mentioned in the *Taming of the Shrew*, Act iv, sc. 1, line **42**.

Jack boy !

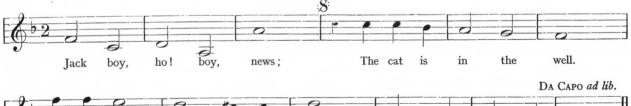

The sign 𝄋 shows where the second voice should begin at "Jack;" the third and fourth follow similarly. This is written straight on, on one stave, in the old style. If Grumio can sing, he should, of course, quote the notes of this Catch, thus—

CURTIS.—"There's fire ready; and therefore, good Grumio, the news."
GRUMIO.—

CURWEN

Hey ho! nobody at home!

Requires five voices, but can be done with four or three.   Printed 1609.

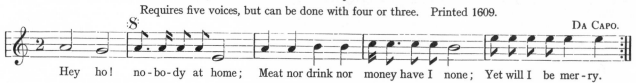

Hey   ho!   no-bo-dy at home;   Meat nor drink nor   money have I   none;   Yet will I   be mer-ry.

As before, the 𝄋 shows where the second voice begins at Hey; consequently a new voice begins at the first beat of every bar throughout, and the result will be a constant alternation of two chords, viz.—

A minor and E minor.

The student will observe that a similar alternation is found in many ancient "part-songs," *e.g.*—

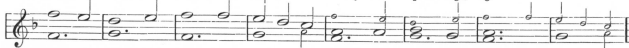

which is of the 13th century, and shows a constant alternation of two chords, F major and G minor; or this—

etc.

which is of the 16th century, and shows the same general idea of harmony.   Popular songs of modern times frequently have a very small number of harmonies, *e.g.*, an alternation of the tonic harmony (*Do*) with the dominant harmony (*Sol*) is often sufficient.   But the alternations given above are quite different; and such differences make the great difficulty in the way of music lovers who wish to understand old music.   These alternations are the consequence of the *Modes*: whereas our modern notions of harmony are related to our conception of *Scales*, major or minor, which were not, save dimly, thought of even, up to the 16th century.

We proceed to the other songs in *Twelfth Night*, Act ii, sc. 3.   The next is "Peg-a-Ramsey," and affords a good illustration of what has just been touched upon, about *key* and *mode*, for it begins on D and ends on C, a course which no modern tune would think of taking.

Peg-a-Ramsey.

Words by E.W.N.

Harmonies by E.W.N.
Tune as given by Mr Wooldridge.

Brightly

PIANOFORTE.

1. Peg-gy   is   a   pret-ty   lass and   cle-ver   with   her   hands   And

CURWEN

well she earns a liv - ing off the things she un - der - stands, For when the Ram - sey shep - herd lad has trou - ble with the lambs He of - ten gets the best of help of bon - ny Peg - a - Ram - sey.

RITORNELLO.✢

V. S.
V. 2.

✢ The *ritornello* may be used as a Dance, *e.g.*, the Coranto steps as given above to Arbeau's little tune (p. 13). The four *minims* in Arbeau's Coranto correspond to the four *crotchets* in Peg-a-Ramsey.

2. Peg-gy is a jol-ly lass and nim-ble on her feet, And when she skips an

Ir-ish jig her steps are bad to beat, And when the clum-sy shepherd lad has

slither'd on his hams He of-ten gets a helping hand of bon-ny Peg-a-Ram-sey.

RITORNELLO.

V. S.
V. 3.

3. Peg-gy is a cheer-y lass and mer-ry in her eye And cer-tain sure the

shep-herd will be hap-py by and bye, For soon as he can fin-ish with the

rams and lambs and dams He wont be long to go to church with bon-ny Peg-a-Ram-sey.

RITORNELLO. *Faster.*

The Dance may be prolonged as desired, by using the various arrangements from v. 2 onward, repeating the sections of the Ritornello between vs. 2 and 3, so as to make 16 bars of it.

CURWEN

8294

Another set of words "sung to" the tune of Peg-a-Ramsey, on quite a different subject, viz., wifely jealousy, is given by Mr. Wooldridge in his edition of Chappell (1893). Curiously the third verse of these words speaks pointedly about "yellow hose," which tempts one to connect them with Malvolio's "yellow stockings;" and if there were any reason to suppose that they were known in Shakespeare's time, Sir Toby's words "Malvolio's a Peg-a-Ramsey" would be explained as meaning that Malvolio was "a jealous fellow who wore yellow stockings." The connection would be quite clear enough to Sir Toby, who was already not particularly sober. Here are the alternative words—

1 When I was a bachelor I led a merry life,
But now I am a married man, and troubled with a wife.

2 I cannot do as I have done, because I live in fear;
If I go but to Islington, my wife is watching there.

3 Give me my *yellow hose* again, give me my *yellow hose*,
For now my wife she watcheth me, see yonder where she goes.

Next to Peg-a-Ramsey, Sir Toby very reasonably thinks of—

Three Merry Men be we.

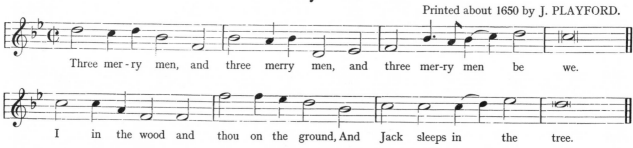

This first verse is from Peele's "Old Wives' Tale," 1595. A second verse, which may be part of the same song, is taken from Fletcher's "Bloody Brother." Fletcher died in 1625. I have put these two verses together, and arranged the tune so as to make a three-part song, such as Sir Toby, Sir Andrew, and the Clown might sing together here.

Three Merry Men be we.

CURWEN

Three merry boys, and three merry boys, and three mer-ry boys are we. As
tree. Three merry boys, and three merry boys are we, mer-ry boys are
tree, sleeps in the tree. Three merry boys are we, merry boys are

ev-er did sing in a hempen string, Un-der the gal-lows tree.
we, as ev-er did sing in a hempen string, sing un-der the gal-lows tree.
we, as ev-er did sing in a hempen string, sing un-der the gal-lows tree.

Sir Toby's next allusion to the popular songs of his time is to the *Ballad of Constant Susanna*. His expression "Tillyvally" is nothing but a piece of impudent rudeness, corresponding to the Cockney "Garn". A rather coarse song by Skelton, set for three men's voices by William Cornysshe, of Henry VII's time, uses the same word, where a drunken fellow is molesting some girl, and the latter gives him a rough tongue in reply, "Tullyvally straw, let be, I say." There is some evidence that the *Ballad of Constant Susanna* was sung to a corrupt version of the tune called "Greensleeves." It does not fit particularly well, but that was no final reason in old days for not using a tune.

Constant Susanna.

Set to Greensleeves (see *Merry Wives of Windsor.* II. i. 60.)

There dwelt a man in Bab-y-lon, Of re-put-a-tion

great by fame: He took to wife a fair wo-man, Su-san-na she was

N.B.—The small notes in the accompaniment, p. 22, bars 3, 4, 7, show the complete tune of "Greensleeves." They may be played or not, as desired.

I have written the harmonies which a person of Henry VIII's day would expect. The *bass* has four notes, viz., *la, sol, la, mi,* just like the first phrase of the Catch "Hey ho, nobody at home." The result is that there is constant alternation between a chord of E minor and a chord of D major, relieved occasionally by a chord of B major. That is, there are only three chords, La, Sol, and occasionally Mi. This is another good example of pre-Shakespearian harmony.

When Malvolio enters (Act ii, sc. 2, line 87) to remonstrate with Sir Toby for making a public house of Olivia's mansion, he tells him straight that if Sir Toby is ready to go, the lady would be very willing to see the last of him.

This reminds Toby of Robert Jones's song "Farewell, dear love," published 1600, a year before the play itself. Toby sings the song with various alterations of the words; which we may explain as another symptom of intoxication.

Farewell Dear Love.
No. XII of "First Booke of Songs and Ayres"

First I give it as Sir Toby and the Clown would use the music in the play.

ROBERT JONES. 1600.

After which Toby returns to Malvolio's unintentional insult of line 92; *apropos* of this last excellent performance, "*Out of time?* Sir, ye *lie!*"

CURWEN

Farewell Dear Love.

In its original form, as a part song with Lute accompaniment.

Translated from the
tablature by E.W.N.
ROBERT JONES 1600.

TREBLE.
Fare-well dear love, since thou wilt needs be gone, mine eyes do shew my
Fare-well, fare-well; since this I find is true, I will not spend more

ALTO.
Fare-well dear love, since thou wilt needs be gone, mine eyes do shew my
Fare-well, fare-well; since this I find is true, I will not spend more

TENOR.
Fare-well dear love, since thou wilt needs be gone, mine eyes do shew my
Fare-well, fare-well; since this I find is true, I will not spend more

BASS.
Fare-well dear love, since thou wilt needs be gone, mine eyes do shew my
Fare-well, fare-well; since this I find is true, I will not spend more

LUTE.

sic.

life is al-most done   Nay I will ne-ver die   so long as I can   spy,
time in woo-ing you;   But I will seek elsewhere if I may find love there.

life is al-most done   Nay I will ne-ver die   so long as I can   spy,
time in woo-ing you;   But I will seek elsewhere if I may find love there.

life is al-most done   Nay I will ne-ver die   so long as I   can spy,
time in woo-ing you;   But I will seek elsewhere if I may find   love there.

life is al-most done   Nay I will ne-ver die   so long as I can   spy,
time in woo-ing you;   But I will seek elsewhere if I may find love there.

① Note carefully that there is only *one flat* in the signature. Therefore do not sing E flat, but E natural, in bars 2 and 4 and elsewhere.

② A. T. B. all have "yet," instead of "nay," in the old printed copy.

CURWEN

8294

There be ma-ny mo', tho'that she do go, There be many mo', I fear
Shall I bid her go? What an if I do? Shall I bid her go and spare

There be ma-ny mo', tho'that she do go, There be many mo', I fear not.
Shall I bid her go? What an if I do? Shall I bid her go and spare not?

There be ma-ny mo', tho'that she do go, There be many mo', I fear not.
Shall I bid her go? What an if I do? Shall I bid her go and spare not?

There be ma-ny mo', tho'that she do go, There be many mo', I fear, I fear
Shall I bid her go? What an if I do? Shall I bid her go and spare, and spare

not, Why then, let her go, I care not.
not? O no, no, no, no, no, I dare not.

Why then, let her go, I care not.
O no, no, no, no, no, I dare not.

Why then, let her go, I care not.
O no, no, no, no, I dare not.

not, Why then, let her go, I care not.
not? O no, no, no, no, I dare not.

Sir Toby uses words from both these two verses. Three more verses may be found in Percy's Reliques, Bohn's edition, 1892, vol. i, p. 151. If it is desired to use this as a song, the singer will take the treble part, and the pianoforte will play the lute part, using the soft pedal, and playing most of the chords *arpeggiando*, which will give some idea of the lute. A bass or contralto voice might sing the melody in E minor, *i.e.*, a minor 3rd lower, in which case the guitar might be used to represent the lute, with which it has considerable affinity. It would begin thus—

VOICE

Farewell dear love, since thou wilt needs be gone Mine eyes do shew my life is al-most done etc.

GUITAR ①

① The guitar sounds an octave lower than written, so play this an octave lower if the pianoforte is used. **CURWEN**

"Come away, Death," sung by the Clown in *Twelfth Night*, Act ii, sc. 4, is described by the Duke as "old and plain." Unfortunately it seems to be lost. Almost the same applies to the song "I am gone, sir," at end of Act iv, sc. 2, though a worthless phrase, probably of the 18th century, does exist, applied to these words. Another song that has vanished is "O! the twelfth day of December," Act ii, sc. 3, line 85.

Hey Robin, jolly Robin.

Twelfth Night, Act iv. sc. 2.

But the original setting of the song sung by the Clown in a spirit of mischief to poor Malvolio, shut up in a dark room, is preserved in a splendid MS. volume of Henry VIII's time, in the British Museum. (Add. MSS. 31922, containing many instrumental pieces, ballads, etc., by various composers such as Cornysshe, Fardinge, Daggere, Kempe, and many pieces by the King Henry VIII himself.) "Hey Robin" is by Cornysshe. First I give the music as the Clown would give it, singing outside the door behind which Malvolio lies in durance, Act iv, sc. 2, line 75—

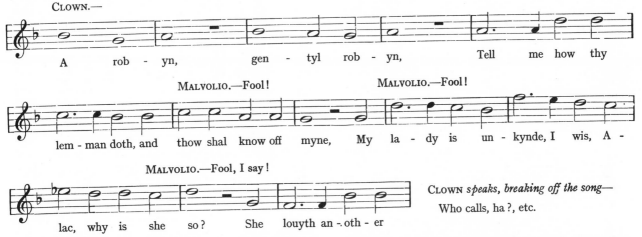

I give the words in the old spelling, *e.g.*, "A robyn"= Hey, Robin; also "louyth"=loveth; and "lemman" in bar 6 simply means a "lover," not in any bad sense, and is used for the lady as well as the man in the case. However, "Hey, Robin" in its original form is not a song, but a sort of Catch, and requires at any rate three voices, though four persons are employable, for the alto part seems to involve two different characters, who answer each other, while the tenor and bass simply repeat their "Round" again and again.

A robyn, gentyl robyn.

Twelfth Night. Act IV. sc. ii. l. 75.
From Brit: Mus: Add. M.S. 31922. Fol. 54.

Music by William Cornysshe
Early XVI century

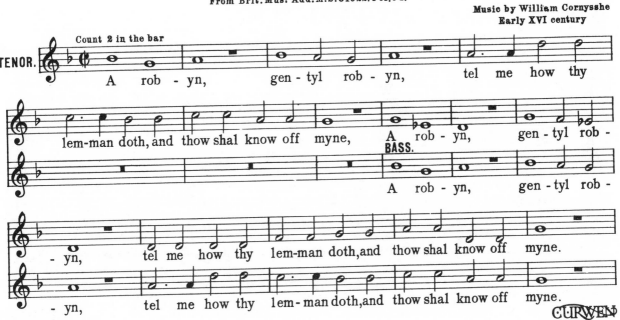

26

Another singer takes this sentence, and the original singer resumes at "alac"; while the former continues at "she louyth another," etc., in dialogue form. There is, of course, no need to do this, if only three voices are available.

CURWEN

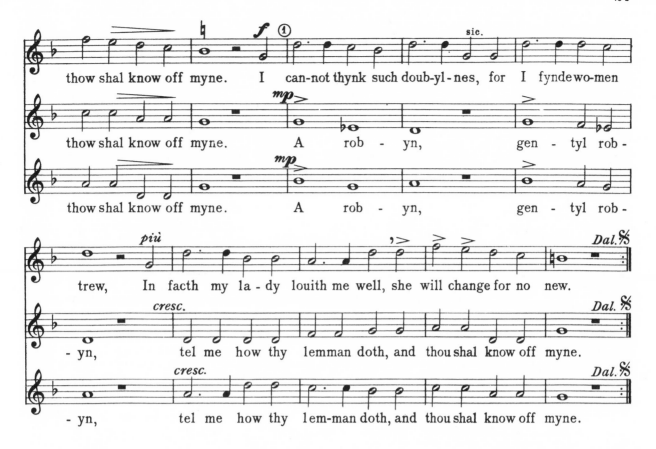

thow shal know off myne. I can-not thynk such doub-yl-nes, for I fynde wo-men

thow shal know off myne. A rob - yn, gen - tyl rob-

thow shal know off myne. A rob - yn, gen - tyl rob-

trew, In facth my la - dy louith me well, she will change for no new.

- yn, tel me how thy lemman doth, and thou shal know off myne.

- yn, tel me how thy lem-man doth, and thou shal know off myne.

Other verses, given in Percy's Reliques, Bohn ed., 1892, vol. i, p. 133, can be adapted if desired. One is inserted as above. The composition has to come to an end, *ad placitum*, when the three voices are all at the words "thou shal know off myne." Three boys can sing it quite comfortably, or three tenors; there is no need to have either bass or alto voices, though, perhaps, A.T.B. would be best. Even then the alto would have to be an old-fashioned counter-tenor to do his part justice. There seems no contemporary setting of the Clown's song at end of *Twelfth Night*—"When that I was," etc.

① The MS. employs a tenor clef here, instead of the alto clef; which shows that yet another man may sing this verse, the two lower voices continuing, as before, to repeat the "Round."

HAMLET.

Act i, sc. 4. The King's drinking party behind the scene, and the King's toast marked by "kettledrum and trumpet." Here is a specimen of the "Flourish" which Hamlet and his friends heard.

From Mr. J. A. KAPPEY'S "Military Music".

The trumpets in the 16th and 17th centuries were all in D, so this would sound a tone higher. But if our modern cornets are available, this flourish will sound quite well, if all use the Bb crook. It will sound satisfactory even if the 4th and 3rd parts are omitted, but the 1st and 2nd are essential, also the drums. If bugles only are to be had, the flourish would have to be altered thus—

The two kettledrums must, of course, be tuned according to the key in use, e.g., for the cornets in Bb, or the bugles, the two notes would be Bb and low F.

Hamlet, Act ii, sc. 2, l. 372, a flourish of trumpets announces the arrival of the company of actors. It was the custom in Shakespeare's time for the trumpets to sound three times before a play began. Near the end of the same scene, line 504, after the First Player has spouted thirty lines at Hamlet's request, old Polonius impolitely observes "This is too long." Hamlet answers a fool according to his folly, suggesting that Polonius' beard wants cutting as much as the actor's lines, and excuses the old man's rudeness to the player in the words, "He's for a jig . . . or he sleeps." Here I give a translation of such a Jig as would have pleased Polonius sufficiently to keep him awake.

Kemp's Jigg.

From the tablature of the Cambridge Lute Book Dd.ii 11.

Transl. E.W.N.

About bar 5 the MS. is inaccurate in time notation and barring. I have written tails up and down in this strange way, e.g., bars 2, 3, 4, to show the student how the tune picks its way over several strings. See below—

The six notes to which the lute strings are tuned in this piece are—

The fingerboard was cut up into semitones, just as is the case with the banjo or guitar. Thus the first chord is easily played; the bass F is string No. 4, the tenor, which is C above, is fingered on string 3, fret 3; the alto F is fingered on string 2, also 3rd fret; and the treble A

is fingered on string 1, fret 2. Anyone who plays the guitar can manage such a piece as this, as it stands, by a slight alteration in the tuning, if necessary. The guitar is usually tuned to these notes.—

thus only No. **3** is different from the lute tuning generally used in Shakespeare's day; and if this G is lowered to F♯, no difficulty can arise. "Kemp's Jigg" on the guitar would read thus, sounding, of course, an octave lower.

Transcr E.W. N.

This Kemp may have been the William Kempe who acted in Shakespeare's plays during Shakespeare's own life. William Kempe was known as a great *dancer*. But

it is quite likely to be composed by the Kempe of Add. MSS. 31922.

CURWEN

Hamlet, Act iii, sc. 2, line 90. The King and Queen, etc., enter the hall to see the play. A "Danish March" is played as they appear. In illustration I give, from the Cambridge Lute Book, Dd ii, 11, 13th page from the end of MS.—

The Hamburgh March.

Transl. E.W. N.

① The two C's are tailed up and down to show that two strings are employed to ensure repetition.
② About here the MS. is inaccurate.

CURWEN

This could be arranged for a band quite easily. In this style for pianoforte, and two cornets (if available). Drums can play the rhythms indicated in the left hand piano stave, *or* play the drum march, given later on, with this (see p. 41).

The Hamburgh March.

Lively.

Arr. E.W. N.

I have taken the liberty of joining the last sections together, so as to make four-bar repeats instead of the two-bar repeats given in the Lute MS. I have written the parts for the two cornets, so as to imitate exactly what the old trumpet could play; and no notes are introduced except those which Shakespeare would hear on *real trumpets pitched in C*. If real trumpets *in D*, which was the regular key in the old days, can be had, they must read all the notes one note lower, and the piano must play the whole thing a tone higher.

 alternative for last two bars.

CURWEN

The King and Queen, Hamlet and Ophelia, etc., take their seats, and the Overture is performed, "Hautboys play." Here is a short piece for "Hautboys" by a Frenchman of Shakespeare's time, Henry Le Jeune.

Pavane in 6 parts, for Hautboys.

LE SIEUR HENRY LE JEUNE.

I have written the 1st hautboy part separately, as it crosses the 2nd so often as to make it impossible to follow in the pianoforte arrangement. The six parts are fairly clear, and could be written out for a small reed band. What would sound most like the "hautboy" band of Shakespeare's time, would be 2 oboes, 2 cors Anglais, 2 bassoons, one instrument for each of the six parts; but this is not likely to be available. But the two middle parts might be played on clarinets, which could easily be got. Le Sieur Henry himself was not very particular, for even in this very piece he suggests that the Basse Taille (*i.e.*, the lowest part but one) may be played on the *sacquebute* (the trombone). In the event of no proper instruments being at hand, the piece might be played on a harmonium, as loud as possible, using the stops called Flûte, Cor Anglais, Hautbois, Basson.

CURWEN

Hamlet, Act iii, sc. 2, line 293. After the Poison Play, Hamlet calls for "some music," which comes (line 345) in the shape of a band of "Recorders," otherwise flutes played with a whistle mouth, something like flageolets.

They were known in France as *Flûtes douces,* because of their sweet tone. Here is such a piece as Hamlet's Recorders would play.

Gavotte for 4 Recorders.

HENRY LE JEUNE.

The only flutes that still remain in use are the various transverse kinds, such as the orchestral flute and piccolo, the military flutes in B♭ and F, etc. None of these can play lower than middle C, so a good deal of the above short piece is out of their reach. It might be arranged for three ordinary flutes, thus—

Arr. E.W.N.

Or the brass "flageolets" sold at the music shops might be used to give some notion of the recorders.

Arr. E.W.N.

This arrangement will be rather too high in pitch, but it is as low as can be got on brass "flageolets," and will sound thus if correctly done—

PIANOFORTE—

etc.

It is a curious fact, that owing to the peculiar *timbre* of these brass "flageolets," their pitch sounds lower than it actually is, unless played with the pianoforte, which shows them up at once. These flageolets should be bought together, to make sure they are made to the same pitch. Particular care should be taken that their scale is in good tune, and that the *fa* of the B♭ instrument is exactly the same note as the *do* of the smaller whistle in E♭. I have transferred the last four bars of the 1st flute part to the 2nd, and *vice versa*, in order to make the parts a little more interesting. If an *organ* is available (not a harmonium or "American," but a real organ), the original arrangement given above, for pianoforte, may be played on a flute stop. An old-fashioned "Stopped Diapason" or "Rohr Flöte" would sound rather like the Recorders which Shakespeare was thinking of. If the stop is a Harmonic Flute 4 feet, play all an octave lower.

Mr. Christopher Welch, in his *Lectures on the Recorder*, gives excellent pictures of Recorders (p. 164), and a picture (p. 167) showing how the player would hand the instrument to Hamlet, when the Prince asks to look at one. The recorder should be offered with the whistle mouth towards Hamlet, so that when he takes it, all the holes are visible. and Hamlet can point to them as he says (Act. iii, sc. 2, line 358) "Govern these ventages" (the finger holes) "with your finger and thumb," etc. The words "and thumb" would not be appropriate to brass "flageolets," which have only the six holes in front, and none at the back. The word "stops" as used by Hamlet (line 361) means the particular combinations of fingering which would produce certain notes. At the end of this speech

(line 371) Hamlet compares himself with a lute, instead of a flute, saying "Call me what instrument you will (let us say a lute, with its great assemblage of strings, so difficult to keep in tune), though you can *fret* me (*i.e.*, you can fix the bits of metal or bone on the neck, which mark the semitones on the fingerboard), you cannot *play* upon me;" thus admonishing Guildenstern that, as the repairer of musical instruments is inferior to the great artist who plays on them, so he has but shown himself a mere artisan vainly attempting to "pluck out the heart of a mystery" which is beyond him, viz., the mystery of Hamlet's own character, whose complexities demand genius in him who would unravel.

We next come to the songs of Ophelia in the Fourth Act of *Hamlet*. The first goes to the old tune of "Walsingham," and the words Ophelia sings are scraps from an old ballad similar to that in the Percy Folio MS., vol. iii, p. 471 (published, Trübner, 1868), which has such lines as—

> "How shold I know your true love,
> That have met many a one," etc.

The old ballad in the Percy Folio is a dialogue between a lover who has lost his love, and a pilgrim whom he meets returning from Walsingham, a shrine which was much cultivated in Henry III's day (say 1241), and onward to the time of Henry VII, who made his pilgrimage to Walsingham from Norwich at Christmas, 1486-7. Catherine of Arragon, when dying, commended her soul to Our Lady at Walsingham; and so did her sometime husband. The priory was dissolved in 1538, and the image of Our Lady burned at Chelsea. Percy's Reliques gives (vol. i, p. 313)

a ballad of Walsingham beginning—

"As ye came from the holy land
    Of blessed Walsingham,
O met you not with my true love
    As by the way ye came.

"How should I know your true love,
    That have met many a one,
As I came from the holy land,
    That have both come and gone?"

Another begins—

"As I went to Walsingham,
    To the shrine with speede,
Met I with a jolly palmer
    In a pilgrimes weed," etc.

Both these go well to the tune "Walsingham," and so do the three verses which Ophelia sings in *Hamlet*, Act iv, sc. 5. Here is the plain tune, as Ophelia might use it—

Rather slow.

1. How should I   your   true   love   know   From an - oth - er   one?
2. He is   dead   and   gone, la - dy,   He is   dead   and   gone;
3. White his shroud as the moun - tain snow, Lard-ed with sweet flowers;

By his cock - le hat and staff, And his sand - al shoon.
At his head a grass - green turf, At his heels a stone.
Which be - wept to the grave did go, With true love showers.

Ophelia's song, tune "Walsingham."

Words by
THOMAS DELONEY.   Words from the Percy Folio M S.   Arr. E.W.N

Not too fast.

VOICE.

PIANOFORTE.

f like a lament.   *p*

1. As yee came ffrom the hol - y land of Wals - ing - ham
2. How shold I know your true love, that have mett many a one,

p

poco marcato il basso.

Da Capo.

mett you not with my true love by the way as you came.
as I came ffrom the ho - ly land, that have come, that have gone?

p

The change from C♮ to C♯ in this tune is very remarkable. I have imitated William Byrd and John Bull, contemporaries of Shakespeare, both of whom set this tune for the virginals, and both, curiously, begin by playing the first phrase alone, without harmony. The bass given above, from the words *poco marcato*, is in imitation of the voice part, and is just what Elizabethan composers would do. The settings by Byrd and Bull are in the printed edition of the Cambridge Fitzwilliam Book (Breitkopf, vol. i, pages 1 and 267). A recent book by Mr. F. Oscar Mann shows these verses are by *Thomas Deloney*, a contemporary ballad maker of Shakespeare's time.

Here is an alternative accompaniment to relieve the first.

Several more verses may be fitted to the tune, thus—

Omit 2 stanzas and conclude,—

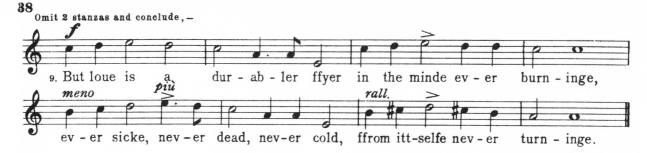

9. But loue is a dur - ab - ler ffyer in the minde ev - er burn - inge,

ev - er sicke, nev - er dead, nev - er cold, ffrom itt-selfe nev - er turn - inge.

This song may be sung by two persons in alternate verses; except that **7** and **8** are taken by the first character, and the last stanza, **9**, by the second, who denies the views held by the first speaker. The *ritornello* may be omitted wherever the singers please, *e.g.*, **7** and **8** should run on.

Also see "The Friar of Orders Gray," in the Percy Reliques, where other reminiscences of Ophelia are collected, which she sings between lines 160 and 200 of this scene.

A corrupt version of "Walsingham," which has been in use on the stage, is given in my "Shakespeare and Music," p.196.

Ophelia's 2nd Song.

Act IV sc.5 line 47.

Arr. E. W. N.
Date uncertain.

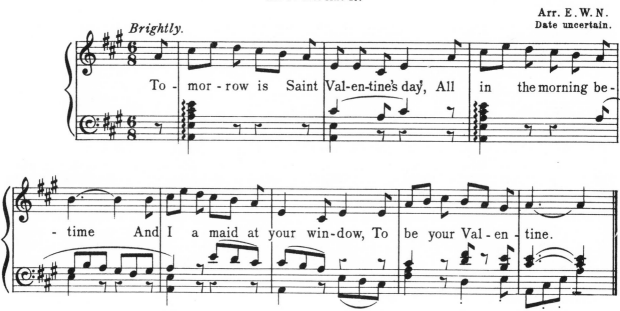

Brightly.

To - mor - row is Saint Val-en-tine's day, All in the morning be -

- time And I a maid at your win-dow, To be your Val - en - tine.

The rest of the words are in Shakespeare. Here is Ophelia's 3rd reminiscence, line 163, which *may* go to the following—

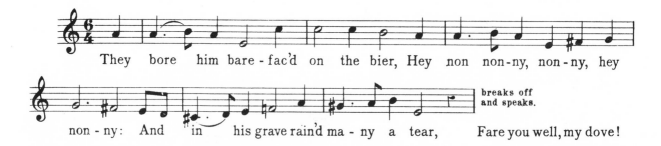

They bore him bare - fac'd on the bier, Hey non non-ny, non-ny, hey

breaks off
and speaks.

non - ny: And in his grave rain'd ma - ny a tear, Fare you well, my dove!

Ophelia's 4th song, "Bonny sweet Robin," line 183. Scarcely anything remains of this song, save the tune "Robin," and one line of words which Ophelia quotes. I have written two verses, including this line, which may be used to the tune, which Shakespeare certainly knew. There is indeed another old line, "My Robin is to the

greenwood gone," but it is not certain whether it belongs to the song Ophelia is thinking of; however, I have used it to begin with. For contemporary settings of "Robin" for virginals, see the Cambridge Fitzwilliam Book, vol. i, p. 66 (John Munday), and vol. ii, page 77 (Giles Farnaby).

CURWEN

Robin.

OPHELIA No 4.

Words by
E. W. N.

Accompt. by E. W. N.

1. My Rob - in is to the green - wood gone, My Rob - in has left me quite a - lone. Sad are the days, a - las, slow - ly the hours do pass: Bon - ny sweet Rob - in is all my moan.

2. My heart is sore with all an - noy, My thoughts are set in one em - ploy. Weep - ing I grieve for him, All would I leave for him: Bon - ny sweet Rob - in is all my joy.

N.B. The B's are all ♮.
There is no ♭ in the signature.

Da Capo.

8294

CURWEN

Notice how the old bass *La Sol La Mi*, already alluded to, finds a prominent place here. Also the contrapuntal treatment at "Sad are the days," which was the usual thing in the 16th century. Likewise the "false relation" in the bar before "sad," was frequently used (F♯ in alto, with F♮ in bass following it). I fear that the introduction, although consisting merely of the characteristic bass notes *La Sol La Mi*, is scarcely Shakespearian, though it might pass as a hint of a "ground," as it was called. This "Robin" would sound beautiful as a quartet, (1) The soprano singer, and (2), (3), (4), a violin, a viola, and a violoncello, playing the alto, tenor, and bass. Or it could be used as a string quartet, without any voice at all, and *danced to* as a Galliard.

Ophelia's last song in Act IV.

Accompt. by E.W.N.

I have written this accompaniment as for the guitar, which would give a fair notion of the lute. When the accompaniment is played on the pianoforte, the soft pedal may be used throughout, and the chords played *arpeggiando*, so as to imitate the lute or guitar. The *Ped.* marks are, of course, meant for pianists only. Most of this accompaniment can be played by a solo *violoncellist*. If this could be had, the effect would be similar to what was often done on the *viol da gamba*, which was used as a song accompaniment, much as the lute; the great difference being that the *viol da gamba* was played with a bow, but the lute with fingers only.

Hamlet, Act v, sc. 1, I know of no contemporary music to the Gravediggers' Song.

Sc. 2, line 291: *Trumpets sound*, see the "flourish" given on p. 28.

CURWEN

Hamlet, Act v, sc. 2, lines 356 and 369, the march heralding Fortinbras, Prince of Norway, may be represented by the "Hamburgh March" given on p. 31; but it is quite as likely to have been simply a drum march, like the one revived in 1610. The authorized copy of this very old English drum march is somewhat uncertain, and I believe not trustworthy. Here, however, is my own impression of what it means.

Ancient English Drum March.

E. W. N.
Revised from the authorized copy of 1610.

This should be begun *ppp*, at line 356, and go on getting very gradually louder right through Hamlet's dying speech; then as soon as Horatio says "Flights of angels sing thee to thy rest," the drums should make a sudden *crescendo*, and play the final bar exactly as Fortinbras enters, and says "Where is this sight?" The March is just the right length for  this purpose; but if it is necessary to make it longer, the ℁ shows where to repeat. N.B.—These drum parts will fit to the "Hamburgh March," if required; using the "Voluntary" as part of the March, there will be 24 bars, and as there are 48 bars in the "Hamburgh March," the drums would play this twice, and then play the final bar by themselves.

CURWEN

MISCELLANEOUS SONGS DUETS & DANCES.

Callino Casturame.

Corruption of Irish, *cailín óg*, "youthful maiden," *a stóirín mín*, "O dearest sweetheart." This old song is mentioned in *Henry V*, Act. iv, sc. 4, line 4. The egregious Pistol uses it as an insult to the French soldier, who was a gentleman, and whose clothes and personal appearance may have seemed effeminate to the dirty rogue who once served Falstaff. First I give it as arranged for Cittern (see *Love's Labour's Lost*, v, 2, 600-603.) from the Cambridge Lute Book, Dd. iv, 23, page 35.

The MS. calls this "Callino Robinson." [There is another quite different tune called "Callino" on p. 44 of the MS.]

These harmonies should be compared with those given on p. 16, just before Peg-a-Ramsey. The Cittern had four double strings, as a mandoline has. The tuning was designed to make the usual chords very easy, *e.g.*, in the above example the three principal chords of C major, F major, and D major are played with just *one* fret each. The four pitches in this piece are—

1st, 2nd, 3rd, 4th.

The version of this melody as given by William Byrd (Fitzwilliam Book, piece clviii) is somewhat different, and as the Lute Book form fits the first words best, I have given both.

Callino Casturame.

Giving a selection of the words printed in 1584.

Arr. E.W.N.

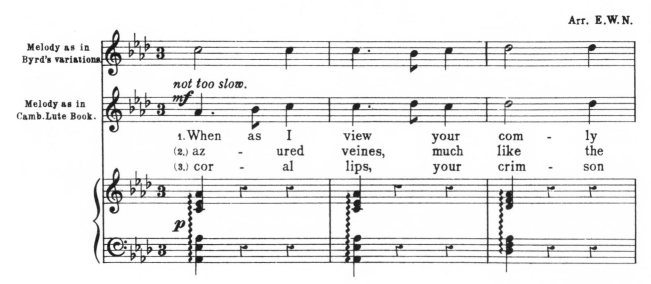

grace, Cal - en - o Cus - tu - re -
skies, Cal - en - o Cus - tu - re -
cheekes, Cal - en - o Cus - tu - re -

- me, Your gold - en haires, your an - gel's
- me, Your sil - ver teeth, your chris - tal
- me, That Gods and men both love and

face, Cal - en - o Cus - tu - re - me.
eies, Cal - en - o Cus - tu - re - me. 2.Your
leekes, Cal - en - o Cus - tu - re - me. 3.Your

I omit 6 lines here and pass on to—

CURWEN

somewhat slower and with great feeling.

4. My soule with si - lence mov - ing sense, Cal - en -
5. Long life and ver - tue you pos - sesse, Cal - en -

cresc.

- o Cus - tu - re - me, Doth wish of God with
- o Cus - tu - re - me, To match those gifts of

cresc.

dim. *pp and a little slower.*

rev - er - ence, Cal - en - o Cus - tu - re - me.
wor - thi - nesse, Cal - en - o Cus - tu - re - me.

dim. *pp colla voce.*

The flowing part in this accompaniment for vs. 4 and 5 is quite inexcusable from the historical point of view. But it would sound well, as a violin obbligato, for instance, while the piano would play the same chords as at v. 1, except the last bars of vs. 4 and 5. It is worthy of mention that William Byrd, evidently affected by the final words, completes his sixth variation on this charming tune, with an unmistakable Amen, *viz.:—*

The original of Byrd is in the key of C. Byrd lived from 1543 to 1623.

WILLIAM BYRD.

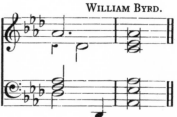

CURWEN

Jon come kisse me now.

Dialogue between husband and wife. Not found
in Shakespeare, but well known in his time.

Arr. E.W.N.

WIFE.
Brightly.

1. Jon come kisse me now, now, Jon come kisse me now. Jon come kisse me

by and by, and mak no mor a - dow. (a - do)

HUSBAND.

2. Peace, I'm an - grie now, now,

peace, I'm an - grie now, Peace, I'm an - grie at the hert, and know not qt to (what)

WIFE. *insinuatingly.*

Jon come kisse me now, Jon come kisse me now,

HUSBAND.

dow. (do)

Peace, I'm an - grie now, Peace, I'm an - grie

CURWEN

*Omit verses 4 and 5. Verse 6 I have put into the wife's mouth to give her a turn.

These several "arrangements" of the old tune are imitations of what was usual during Elizabethan days. The remainder of the words may be found in my "Elizabethan Virginal Book" (Dent, 1905). Of course my "duet" passages may be omitted at pleasure. Do not be afraid of the F♯ and F♮ in the last line, bar 2!

CURWEN

It was a Lover and his Lass.

Sung by the two Pages in *As You Like it*, Act v, sc. 3. The 2nd Page describes the performance as "Like two gipsies on a horse," so I give Thomas Morley's setting arranged as a duet. Thomas Morley's original is in his "First Book of Ayres," published 1600.

Arr. E.W.N.

CURWEN

N.B.—The two voice parts can be used *without* the accompaniment, as they make a complete two-part madrigal in themselves.

N.N.B.—The 2nd voice may be omitted, and the music used as a solo song.

The second, third and fourth verses are in Shakespeare.

Come live with me.

Portions of this song are sung by Parson Hugh in *Merry Wives of Windsor*, Act iii, sc. 1. Parson Hugh is in a very nervous state, and gets the version of Psalm cxxxvii mixed up with Marlowe's *Passionate Pilgrim*, part xx:—"shallow rivers" and "singing" suggesting "Babylon," hence his interpolation at line 26, as he remembers "When as we sat in Babylon, The rivers round about." The *Passionate Pilgrim* is, of course, printed as one of Shakespeare's works. Parson Hugh sings lines from verses 2 and 3 of Part xx, quoting without any great accuracy, however. At the repetition of "fragrant posies," he says "vagram," because he is going to cry, and tears are in his nose.

Arr. E. W. N.

1. Come live with me, and be my love, And we will all the plea-sures prove That hills and val - leys, dale and field And all the crag - gy moun-tains yield.
2. And we will sit up - on the rocks, See - ing the shep - herds feed their flocks By shal - low riv - ers, to whose falls Mel - od - ious birds sing mad - ri - gals.
3. There will I make thee a bed of roses With a thou - sand fra - grant posies, A cap of flow - ers, and a kirtle Im - bro - dred all with leaves of mirtle.

The accompaniment could be performed by violin, viola, and violoncello. Or a single violin might make a good part by playing the *tune* of the introductory six bars, and then the uppermost part in the accompaniment, from the word *espress.*, thus making a duet obbligato with the voice.

CURWEN

Come o'er the Bourn, Bessy, to me.

Edgar quotes this very old song, in his pretended madness, *King Lear*, Act iii, sc. 6, line 25, the Fool supplying extempore words on the hint of Edgar's quotation, "Her boat hath a leak," etc. I have "constructed" the tune from the setting for lute in the Cambridge Lute Book, MSS. Dd. 2, 11, 39 pages from the end of this folio MS. Here is the original, exactly as in the tablature. (Mr. Wooldridge's reference in O.E. Pop. Mus., vol. i, p. 122, is wrong.)

COME OVER THE *BROOME* BESSY.

Transl. E. W. N.

The MS. ends thus, but it would not be possible to stop here; the composer of the setting probably meant either to finish with a big chord of G, or to repeat, and the final bar would lead back to the beginning. There is just as bad a case in Schumann's Carneval. The mark "sic" in the last line refers to the "g," which probably should be "f".

① There is (of course) no flat in the signature, but I mark all B naturals and flats as they come, to prevent any misunderstanding.

CURWEN

Come over the born Bessy.

Early XVI century.
Tune and harmony from the Cambridge Lute Book. M S S.Dd. 2.11.

"King Lear." Act III. sc.6. line 25.

No flat in the signature.

Arr. E.W.N.

Come ov - er the
born Bess, Come ov - er the born Bess, Sweete Bes - sy come
ov - er to me. And I shall thee
take, And my dere la - dy make Be-fore all o - ther that

CURWEN

ev - er I see. My - thinke I hear a voice
(Me - thinks)

At whom I do re - joyce, And aun - swer thee now I

shall. Tel me, I say, What art thou that bids me come a -

- way, And so ear - nest - ly doost me call.
(do - est)

More words given in Wooldridge's Chappell's O.E. Pop. Mus. I. 122.

Alternative accompaniment for last 2
bars, embodying the text of the original
(see above p. 52 last two bars.)

dim e rall.

The final chord, as already explained,
is not in the M S. but is quite probably
what the composer intended.

N.B.—The E. and B. mean England and Queen Bess. These are not the original words belonging to this tune, which is considerably older than "Bessy's" time. The two persons might be represented by two singers, *e.g.*, tenor and soprano.

CURWEN

A SET OF DANCES AS KNOWN TO SHAKESPEARE.

Pavane.

For Cittern.

From Cambridge M S. Lute Book Dd. 14. 24.

By N. STROGERS.

The name Pavane (1) does not occur in Shakespeare, but the thing is often mentioned under the word *Measure, e.g.,* *Henry VIII*, Act i, sc. 4, l. 104; *As You Like it*, Act v, sc. 4, l. 178, etc.

Arr. for Mandolines, or Pianoforte, or both, by E.W.N.

Repeat, reversing all the marks of expression, and if a third repetition is wanted, use a strong accent on the first beat of each bar.

The two mandolines alone will sound not unlike the cittern (*Love's Labour's Lost*, v. 2, 600). Two violins could play this, either with the bow, or *pizzicato*; or, first one and then the other, for a change. The "steps" explained above on page 12, will fit to successive *minims* in this Pavane.

(1) The Passy-measure or pavin of *Twelfth Night*, Act v, sc. 1, l. 197, is the Passamezzo, *i.e.*, the pavan played *much faster*. Sir Toby calls the doctor that, because he had got drunk *too quickly*. See my "Shakespeare and Music," p. 135.

CURWEN

8294

Galliard.

Tune from Arbeau's Orchesographie, ed. 1588.

Arr. E.W.N.

This music will serve for Tourdion, Galliard, Cinque pas, and La Volta. The steps of the Tourdion are similar to those of the Galliard, one movement for each of *six* minims. (1) Pied en l'air droicte; (2) ditto gaulche; (3), (4) same as (1), (2); and at (5) a *sault moyen*; (6) posture droicte; and repeat, reversing *right* and *left*. The leap at (5) is to be a *moderate* one only; and otherwise the Tourdion is danced "low," and therefore at a good speed (*legière et concitée*), whereas the Galliard is danced "high," *e.g.*, the leap at (5) is a *sault majeur*, and thus the speed cannot be so great, but must be *plus lente et pesante*, so as to give time for more active movements. The *Cinq pas de la galliarde* is like the Tourdion, but "higher" and more "virilement," and instead of "pied en l'air," you perform "coups de pied," "ou grèves." The Cinq pas also has the "high" leap or "sault majeur." To illustrate the Cinq pas, see *Much Ado about Nothing*, Act ii, sc 1, line 68, *ff*, where Beatrice compares "wooing, wedding, and repenting" with "a Scotch jig, a measure, and a cinque pace," describing the repentance as falling "into the *cinque pace* faster and faster till he *sink* into his grave." "Sink" is a pun on "Cinque," and I daresay even "grave" is a pun on "grève," which was the technical name of one of the steps allowed in the cinque pas. La Volta, or Lavolt (see *Troilus and Cressida*, Act iv, sc. 4, line 84) goes to the Galliard tune, but, as the dancer had to keep twisting round, there was only time to get in four "steps," in-

cluding the "big leap," thus—where the four movements marked were: (1) Petit pas, en saultant sur le gaulche, pour faire pied en l'air droit. (2) Plus grand pas du droit. (3) Sault majeur (hence "the high lavolt"). (4) Posture en pied joincts; and so on, once every two bars. The meaning seems to be, in simple English: (1) a small leap off the left foot; right foot bounces up a little way. (2) The same, but the right foot springs further into the air. (3) The great leap (*Twelfth Night*, Act. i, sc. 3, line 131, on the "excellent constitution" of Sir Andrew's leg). (4) Come down on both feet; feet together. Add to this a constant "whirl," of which Arbeau's pupil (1588) remarks: "Ces vertigues et tornoiements de cerveau me fascheroient" quite a natural remark in a beginner, who probably got giddy rather easily. Curious woodcuts of "steps" and "postures" used in these dances are given in Arbeau's book; see p. xv, where four of them are reproduced.

The *Coranto* (2) has already been dealt with on p. 13 (see under *Twelfth Night*). Shakespeare's contemporary, Selden, speaks of the Pavane, Galliard, and Coranto, as the ceremonious dances. Those which follow, such as Canaries, Brawl, Haye, were less and less "stately," and more and more noisy, till the lowest depth of "kitchen lancers" was reached (according to Selden) with Trenchmore and the Cushion Dance.

① As before, there is no E♭ in the signature. ② See also Peg-a-Ramsey, p. 16.

CURWEN

The *Canaries* and the *French Brawl* are both mentioned by Moth in *Love's Labour's Lost*, Act iii, sc. 1, line 10, *ff.*

Canaries.

Tune from Arbeau (ed. 1588.)

Arr. E.W.N.

Another harmony for the same tune (the melody may be played on violin or flute).

E.W.N.
Da Capo.

The steps of the Canaries were six in number, one on each separate note of the tune given above. (1) Tap of left foot, resulting in right toe in air. (2) Stamp right heel. (3) Ditto right foot. Steps 4, 5, 6, are the same but the words "left" and "right" change places throughout. Thus, the six steps are accomplished every two bars of the tune, and Lafeu's phrase, in *All's well that ends well*, Act ii, sc. 1, line 76, about the "spritely fire and motion" of the canary dance, would seem more than justified.

The French *Brawl* had many varieties. Here is Arbeau's tune for the *Branle* (Brawl) *des Sabots*.

Branle (Brawl) des Sabots.

Arr. E.W.N.

Steps 1—4 are those of a *Double gaulche*, *i.e.*, left foot forward; bring right foot up to left; left foot forward again; join feet. Steps 5—8 are the same, except "right" and "left" change places. Steps 9—10 are a *Simple gaulche*, *i.e.*, left foot forward; join feet. Steps 11—12 are a *Simple droit*, *i.e.*, right foot forward; join feet. Finally, A, B, C are three taps of the right foot.

58

In *Love's Labour's Lost*, Act v, sc. 1, line 120, the school-master, Holofernes, proposes to get up a Pageant of the Nine Worthies. The constable, Dull (line 148) offers to play the tabor (no doubt with its inseparable "pipe"), and make the Worthies dance "The Hay". Later on, in the second scene, line 486, it appears that there are only three people to take the nine parts. However, three people can dance the Hay. "Haye" is French for "Hedge," and one feature of the "Hay" was that the dancers had to "faire la haye les uns parmy les aultres," that is, "make the hedge, one amongst another." Thus, if three dancers, X Y Z, start in a row, in that order, they have to change places during the first four steps, when Y, instead of being in the middle, will be outside, and the three will be in the order Y X Z. X has made himself a sort of "hedge" (haye) between Y and Z. And so on, during the next four steps Z will find himself between the other two. In fact, it is a sort of "chain." In George Villiers' play *The Rehearsal* (1671) the Hay is danced by Earth, Sun, and Moon, and the Moon is *eclipsed* by the Earth, etc., see Act v, sc. 1.

The Haye.

Tune from Arbeau ed. 1588.

E. W. N.

The steps begin at 1, counting one step to every semi-breve; thus 1, two simples; 2, a double; 3, two simples; 4, a double; 5—8, repeat the same, not forgetting "faire la haye" once in every four steps. This music would go well as a string quartet; a 3rd violin can play the tenor, as the tenor nowhere goes below G. Or a flute might play the tune, and two violins the alto and tenor, with a violoncello, or even the piano, to take the bass. This latter arrangement would be "broken consort." The only place where an *end* can be made is one bar after the 4.

I am a joly foster.(forester)

From Add.M S. 31922. temp.Henry VIII.fol.69.b.

Date early XVI century.

Might be used in"As you like it", Act II, scenes V and VII.

Copied and Edited, E.W.N.

① This three-part song may be sung also by two trebles and an alto. The alto sings the bass an octave higher. A tenor could take the lowest part instead of an alto, except the first sentence, which would have to be sung as written, after that rise an octave.

CURWEN

① "For shote [also spelt *shot* and *shott*] ryght well I may" means "for shoot right well I can." I have slightly rearranged the words here, but have retained the slipshod spelling, as characteristic of the time.

② Gren wod = greenwood.

③ *Ye* is *the*, and is to be pronounced *the*. It is spelt either way indifferently.

④ *Bough*, spelt also *bought*, as also *enought* in the next sentence. Pronounce *enough* to rhyme with *bough*, *i.e.*, *enow*.

⑤ *Lynde*, pronounce long to rhyme with "hynd". *Lynde* = lime tree; used here for *any* tree. *Underlind* meant "in the woods."

⑥ In this verse, about the forester's *horn*, "I can ye deth of a deer," means that he "knows" how to blow "the death" on his horn, *i.e.*, a call, or fanfare, announcing the death of the deer.

* The time-notation of this, and similar bars from here to the end, is in accordance with the original MS. The 1st tenor and the bass must hold on their breves until the middle voice has finished his bar.

CURWEN

⑦ "I can luge and make a fute." *Luge* means "Lodge." To "lodge" a buck is to find the place where the buck "lodges." *Fute*, also spelt *feute*, is the "track" of a beast; so "luge and make a fute" means, to track the deer to his lair. The forester would "lodge" the buck overnight, and "rouse" him next morning.

CURWEN

Ah, the sighs that come from my heart.

Add. MSS. 31922 fol 32.b.

Might be used in *Two Gentlemen of Verona*, Act iv, sc. 2, as part of the Silvia serenade. See Lady Carey's Dump.

E.W.N.
WILLIAM CORNYSSHE. about 1510.

① The part I have called *Alto* is really a *Tenor*, and has the melody.

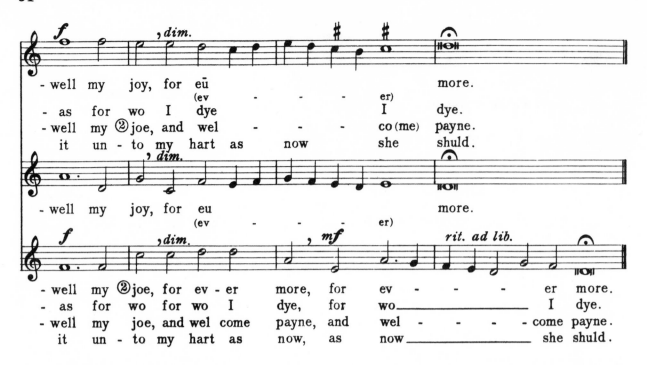

- well my joy, for eū (ev - - - er) more.
- as for wo I dye I dye.
- well my ②joe, and wel - - - co(me) payne.
it un - to my hart as now she shuld.

- well my joy, for eu (ev - - - er) more.

- well my ②joe, for ev - er more, for ev - - - er more.
- as for wo for wo I dye, for wo_____ I dye.
- well my joe, and wel come payne, and wel - - - come payne.
it un - to my hart as now, as now_____ she shuld.

Mr. Wooldridge prints this music in two versions. I give this as the better; and further, because the words of the MS. differ here and there from those given by him, *e.g.*, in v. 1 the MS. has "sen (or sens) ye muft ned' fro' me depart." Mr. Wooldridge gives "syth I must fro' my love depart;" and in v. 4 the MS. gives "as wosto god I could" (as would to God I could); while Mr. Wooldridge has "as wolde to gode that I myghtt."

Green grows the holly.
From the same M S fol 37 b. words of verses 2 to 5 on fol 38 a.

This might be sung at the end of Act I of *King Henry VIII*, where the King calls for music.

E.W.N.
Composed by KING HENRY VIII.

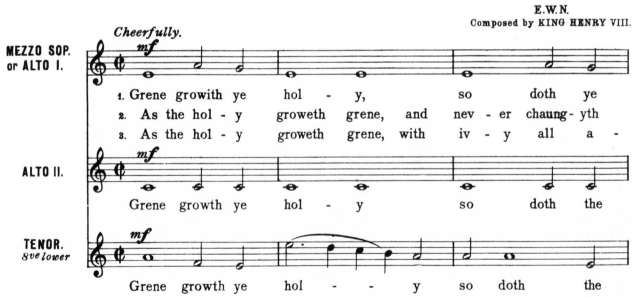

MEZZO SOP. or ALTO I.
1. Grene growith ye hol - y, so doth ye
2. As the hol - y groweth grene, and nev - er chaung - yth
3. As the hol - y groweth grene, with iv - y all a -

ALTO II.
Grene growth ye hol - y so doth the

TENOR. *8ve lower*
Grene growth ye hol - - y so doth the

② "Joe," a form of "joy." Compare "John Anderson, my Jo," and Yorkshire dialect "doy," which was, not long ago, a word of extreme endearment.

CURWEN

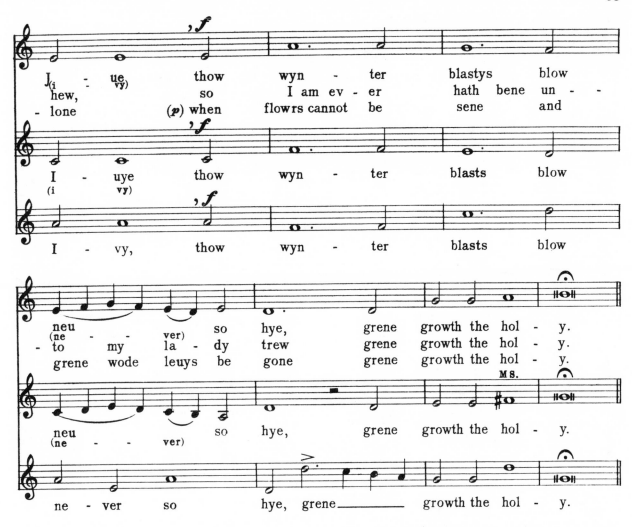

In v. 3 "flowers" is spelt "flowerys" and "leaves" is spelt "leuys." It seems best to alter these. The following transposition, for boys, or men only, has the rest of the words. Long notes must be divided according to the swing of the words, *e.g.*, v. 2.

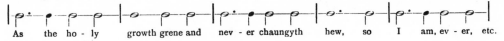

As the ho-ly growth grene and nev-er chaungyth hew, so I am, ev-er, etc.

The same trans-posed for

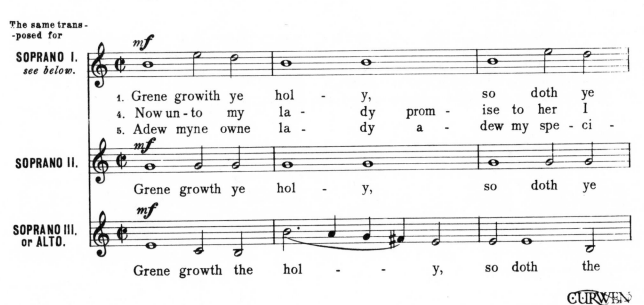

SOPRANO I.
see below.

1. Grene growith ye hol - y, so doth ye
4. Now un-to my la - dy prom - ise to her I
5. Adew myne owne la - dy a - dew my spe - ci -

SOPRANO II.

Grene growth ye hol - y, so doth ye

SOPRANO III.
or ALTO.

Grene growth the hol - y, so doth the

CURWEN

Last verse better so —

A - dew myne owne la-dy, a - dew my spe-ci - all, who hath my hart trew-ly, be   sure,

This latter arrangement, sung an 8ve lower, is suitable for Tenor, Baritone, and Bass. I have modernized the spelling here, as boys cannot be expected to recognize "ivy" in "Iue." The variations in the spelling of single words are left as in MS., *e.g.*, "growith" in top stave, and "growth" elsewhere; "Iue" in top stave, "Iuye" elsewhere, in the men's copy.

In verse 4 "promise" is spelt in abbreviation "proyse."

In verse 5 "speciall"="best girl" in modern slang; "sure" is spelt "suere," and "ever" as usual "eu."

CURWEN

ADDENDA, 1927

P. iv. *William Cornysshe*. Calendar of Patent Rolls—July 13, 1494—grant to W. C., King's servant, of the keeping of one brewhouse and four other messuages in the parish of S. Martin-in-the-Fields by Charyngcrosse, Co. Middlesex [the property of James Nicol, an idiot; W. C. was to feed and clothe J. N. during his idiocy].

Cornysshe went with King Henry to the meeting of the English and French Kings at the 'Field of the Cloth of Gold', in 1519. W. C. devised the pageants at the Banquet (Grove, Appendix, 1889).

P. xv. *Czerwinski, A.* Also wrote *Geschichte der Tanzkunst*, etc., 34 illustrations and 9 old dance tunes. Leipzig 1862, 8vo.

id. *Greue droicte*. See p. 56.

P. 12, l. 27. See p. 56.

P. 13. 'Cobbler's Jig'. This tune is taken from *Bellerophon—of Lust tot Wysheyd* [or, Desire for Wisdom], Amsterdam, 1622. It also appears in *Nederlandtsche Gedenck-Clanck* [Netherlandish memorial-sound], 1626. Here it is called 'Engelslapperken', *i.e.* English cobbler or patcher.

This *Gedenck-Clanck* was in Ellis's catalogue of 1920, £30, in vellum. It contains 70 Dutch songs to the lute and cittern.

In 1916, Mr. R. A. Streatfield (since dead) and Sir Edward Elgar wrote to tell me that a tune almost identical with the 'Cobbler's Jig' is used by Mr. Arthur de Greef in his 'Quatre vielles chansons flamandes' for orchestra, and that he calls it 'The Duke of Alva's statue', with date, 1569.

P. 23. 'Farewell, dear Love'. This tune, slightly corrupted, appears in a Dutch Hymn Book by Kamphuyzen, called *Stichtelyke Rymen* [edifying poems, otherwise pious verse], Amsterdam, 1713.

The first lines of verse 1 are:

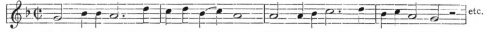

Heyl - gie-rig mensch wiens grond ge-dach - ten   't Ge-niet van lust   en rust be-trach-ten.

'Salvation-greedy man whose deepest thoughts the enjoyment of pleasure and rest consider.'

An earlier edition of *Stichtelyke Rymen*, Amsterdam, 1652, was priced £7 10s. in Ellis's catalogue of 1920.

Another Shakespeare tune, 'Fortune, my Foe', appears on p. 43 of the same book, set to a paraphrase of Psalm cxxix, *i.e.*:

Zy hebben my (zoo zegge Israel)
Van jeuget op door veelderley gequel, etc.

That is: 'Many a time have they fought against me' (Saepe expugnaverunt).

P. 29. *Kemp*. There is a story about Kemp in *Archie Armstrong's Jest Book*. Armstrong was Court Jester to James I and Charles I.

P. 40, r.h. column, 3 lines from the bottom. The words of the Grave-digger's Song in *Hamlet* are by Thomas, Lord Vaux.

P. 52, r.h. column, 2 lines from the bottom. Schumann's 'Carneval,' 'Valse Allemande,' bar 8.

P. 56, l.h. column, 5 lines from the bottom. See pp. xv and 12.